IMAGES
of America

TIN CAN TOURISTS IN
FLORIDA
1900–1970

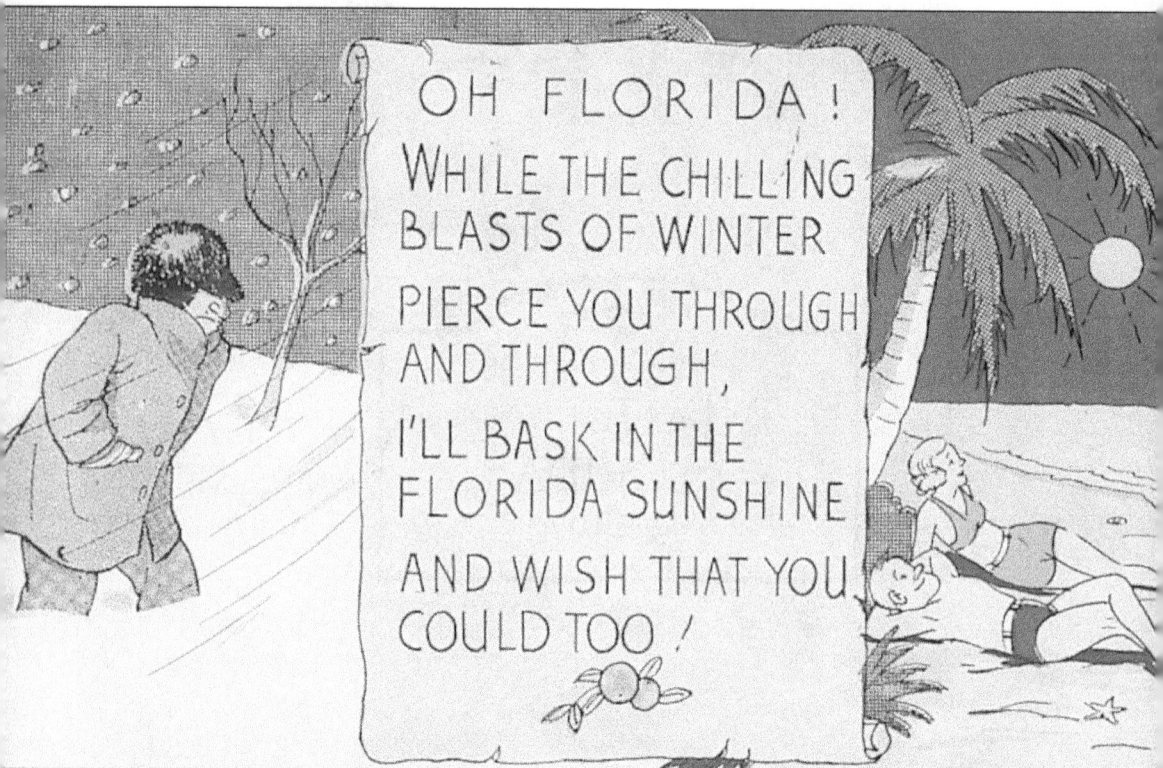

Few Tin Canners could resist sending postal reminders to their friends in the North that Florida offered unlimited sunshine and exotic locales to be enjoyed while Northerners were fighting the rigors of winter.

IMAGES
of America

Tin Can Tourists in
FLORIDA
1900–1970

Nick Wynne

ARCADIA
PUBLISHING

Copyright © 1999 by Nick Wynne.
ISBN 978-1-5316-0140-9

Published by Arcadia Publishing,
Charleston, South Carolina

Library of Congress Catalog Card Number: 99-65056

For all general information contact Arcadia Publishing at:
Telephone 843-853-2070
Fax 843-853-0044
E-Mail sales@arcadiapublishing.com
For customer service and orders:
Toll-Free 1-888-313-2665

Visit us on the Internet at www.arcadiapublishing.com

Look Out Camp near Cassadaga is pictured here in March 1921. This early "woody" provided a means of transportation and served as an extension to the campers' tents. Cassadaga, which has become famous as a town whose population is largely composed of mystics, seers, fortunetellers, and mediums, was a popular camping spot for early motorists.

CONTENTS

INTRODUCTION

The invention of the automobile in Europe in the late 19th century was heralded with little fanfare and much ridicule. Seen primarily as a toy for the very rich, the automobile was not regarded as much of a threat to established forms of transportation, such as the locomotive, steam ships, or even the horse and carriage. Indeed, the phrase "Get a horse!" was frequently hurled at motorists by pedestrians or by outraged horsemen whose animals bolted at the sight and sound of the early auto. Even as late as 1910, automobiles were still considered little more than toys. That, however, was to change rapidly.

Three events occurred in rapid succession and changed the nature of the traveling public forever. First, Henry Ford, a tinkerer and inventor, designed and built an automobile that was simple in design, easily maintained, very reliable, and, most important, cheap to purchase. Ford's "Tin Lizzy" dispelled the notion that the automobile was a toy. The "Ford" proved that automobiles could be used in every-day activities, maintained with less bother than a horse or mule, and could take on and conquer the most forbidding terrain. Not only that, but the automobile could carry passengers and heavy loads for miles without requiring a rest break or having to be fed.

Second, Henry Ford also perfected the assembly-line techniques of mass-produced parts that had first been introduced in the United States by Eli Whitney, Samuel Colt, and other manufacturers. By streamlining the manufacturing process into a linear assembly line and by having required parts delivered to that line when and where needed, Ford was able to take the automobile out of the tinker's garage or the fine craftsman's shop into the realm of huge factories, turning out hundreds of cars in a single day. So revolutionary in concept was the Ford manufacturer process that hundreds of competitors copied his methods and plunged into the market with their "brands."

Each of the new brands offered the public a choice of features, which appealed to its customers. Around this idea of brands and differences emerged entirely new class distinctions, based not on breeding or education or even wealth, but on the "make" of car one owned. Even today, this class system prevails.

World War I was the third factor in moving automobiles from the realm of exotic toys to the mainstay of transportation. Although this great cataclysmic exercise in violence first started as a classic 19th-century war, involving men and animals in frontal assaults, it soon changed as new technologies were employed by both sides in efforts to gain an advantage. Poison gas, machine guns, massive artillery guns, airplanes, tanks, and automobiles rapidly made the conflict the first modern war. With more than two million casualties in a short four-year period, the world became convinced that technology was "the wave of the future."

World War I also ensured that thousands of vehicles, declared surplus when the war ended, would find their way into the hands of individuals around the world. But nowhere did populations more readily accept the automobile than in the United States. Surplus Army vehicles, sold at low prices, were immediately purchased and put to a wide variety of tasks. Old tanks became tractors, ambulances were converted into cargo carriers, and staff cars were turned into family cars. Factories that had supplied these instruments of war now became producers of specialized civilian vehicles. Soon a stream of new tractors, trucks, and cars replaced the aging war-surplus vehicles. Demand outstripped supply, fueled by a postwar economy that boomed, the creation of the "monthly payment" plan, and the influence of a newly emerging Hollywood film industry that glamorized the automobile as an essential element in modern life. Even the criminal elements did their part. Americans were enchanted by news stories about the Barker Gang, Bonnie and Clyde, and countless others who used the automobile to rob banks and to make their getaways. In places like Chicago, the use of automobiles to haul bootleg whiskey or as symbols of wealth added to the growing mystique of the auto.

In addition, the automobile became the symbol of the "New Generation" of Americans that delighted in the mobility and anonymity it provided. No longer were youths restricted by a slow-moving horse-and-buggy or by the straight lines of a railroad. No longer were they forced to live under the watchful eyes of family or acquaintances. The automobile offered the liberating privacy of far horizons and secret places.

But these were not the only uses the public found for the automobile. Just as young Americans saw it as a means of escaping their restricted environment, so, too, did thousands of others of all ages. The great sense of adventure that had pushed Americans from the Atlantic to the Pacific had not vanished with the arrival of the 20th century. Men, women, and children looked upon the automobile as a new way to explore the unknown. No longer was leisure travel reserved for the rich or well-to-do, the automobile brought about a new sense of egalitarianism on the American roads. Throwing a tent in the back or strapping it on top of the car, thousands of Americans set out to explore the backroads of the United States. Carrying extra gasoline in 5-gallon cans, plenty of canned food in sacks, and extra tires strapped to the fenders, these intrepid souls began an exploration of the North American continent with a thoroughness that put Lewis and Clark to shame. They became the symbol of another "New Generation" of Americans, restless, adventuresome, and filled with boundless curiosity. These were the "Tin Can" tourists.

In 1919, the Tin Can Tourists of the World (TCT) was formed in Tampa's DeSota [sic] Park, and from then until 1977, Tin Canners held two annual meetings a year. One meeting was held in Michigan and the other was held in either Tampa, Sarasota, Ocala, or some other Florida location. The creation of this group signaled the maturation of caravanning in the United States and the recognition that those who took to the highways and dirt roads of the nation made up a definite subculture of American society. Although the origins of the name "Tin Can Tourists" are obscure, it quickly gained widespread acceptance. One story has it that the name was derived from "Tin Lizzie," the name given to the automobiles of the period, while another attributes it to the numerous "tinned" food cans that made up a substantial part of the diet of early tourists. Still a third story insisted that the name came from the large cans that held gasoline or water and which were attached at every likely place on the auto. Some members of the group soldered a tin can to their radiator cap as a badge of their participation.

Residents of Florida recognized the potential positive economic impact of the Tin Canners on the state, and the movement to build "Good Roads" spread rapidly throughout Florida. By the mid-1920s, Florida had built almost 900 miles of hard-surfaced highways, while the number of miles of paved roads in 1930 had grown to more than 3,000. The completion of the "Montreal to Miami" highway (the so-called Dixie Highway) in 1915 and the opening of the Tamiami Trail in 1928 set the pattern of what has become almost a full century of highway expansion.

Membership in the association provided a clear distinction between those who traveled for fun and recreation and those who took to the highways for economic reasons. If one looks at pictures of early Tin Canners and the Okies of the late 1920s, it is difficult to distinguish between the two. TCT membership provided that distinction.

The formation of the Tin Can Tourist organization also gave a certain amount of clout to the group, and throughout the nation, municipalities and private individuals established camps to accommodate its members. Throughout the 1930s, 1940s, and early 1950s, these camps flourished with the influx of seasonal visitors who brought their homes with them. Gradually such camps began to diminish in importance as small and affordable motels replaced them in the late 1950s and 1960s. By the mid-1970s and 1980s, the towed "house trailer" had been replaced by self-propelled "recreational vehicles" that were frequently as expensive as permanent family homes in manicured subdivisions. In 1977, the last annual meeting of the Tin Can Tourist of the World was held.

Still the romance of the Tin Can tourist concept lingered on. Sellers of R-Vs found it necessary to provide the same kind of organization and services as those provided by the Tin Can Tourist Association. Today purchasers of recreational vehicles are offered membership in Kampgrounds of America (KOA) or in "Good Sam" clubs. Of course, the American Automobile Association provides many of the services once provided by the TCT.

Although the Tin Canners have been replaced by millions of other visitors using more diverse forms of transportation, they were truly pioneers. This is their book.

Acknowledgments

This book would not have been possible without the support of my wife, Debra, and my father-in-law, Herman Chapin. In addition, the following people gave me use of their postcards and encouraged me in my work: Ada E. Parrish, George Leland Harrell, and Alma Clyde Field.

I also wish to thank the staff of the Tebeau-Field Library of Florida History in Cocoa, the University of South Florida Library Special Collections Department in Tampa, the Florida Archives, and the St. Lucie County Historical Museum. Paul Camp, David Coles, Robert A. Taylor, and Deanna Bonner-Ganter, who organized the Meyer Collection, deserve special thanks.

I also want to thank my children, Lisa and Patrick, who inspire by being.

All royalties from this book will be given to the Tebeau-Field Library of Florida History in Cocoa, FL.

One

Pioneers of the Open Road

The Photographs of Ernest Meyer

The popularity of the automobile quickly exceeded the capabilities of existing paved highways in the nation. In Florida, most of the roads that connected cities and towns were little more than heavily rutted dirt roads, with few bridges and even fewer amenities for the traveler. Some cities featured brick-paved main streets, but even these were few. Tin Canners who set out to explore the countryside frequently encountered swollen streams, fallen timbers, swampy quagmires, and countless other obstacles, little changed from those faced by the pioneers of two centuries earlier.

In the country, the open range laws of the Sunshine State added an element of danger for the speedy automobiles and their passengers. Hogs, cattle, and other livestock roamed freely, using the roads as thoroughfares from one thicket or range to another. As a result, life on the road was hazardous to those who dared explore in a "horseless carriage."

Few places offered lodgings or public campgrounds to the earliest of these tourists, and tents were the order of the day. Often Tin Canners modified their tents to include their automobiles as part of the structure. Thus, the vehicle became a place of rest as well as a mode of transportation.

The precariousness of early automobile travel, the uncomfortable accommodations, and the uncertainly of what lay around the next bend of the road combined to spell adventure. Like the explorers of old, Tin Can tourists knew that whatever route they took, they would escape the tedium of daily life and enjoy the adrenaline rush of exciting new places.

The majority of photographs in this chapter were taken by Ernest Meyer on automobile tours of Florida in 1921–1924. Meyer, his wife Jennie, and a black feline named "Cat" traveled throughout the state. The Meyer photographs are unique and have never been published before, and although some of the glass negatives did not print as clear as had been hoped, they constitute the only known record of some of these early sites.

Pictured here in 1911, Fred Gilbert's garage in Jacksonville was based on providing the same services offered in large train depots to automobile tourists. The garage offered a "Hydraulic plunger elevator, complete shop and charging plant. Elegant show rooms, ladies and gents reception and dressing rooms, and all accommodations for touring parties . . . ."

This picture of an early campground north of Jacksonville is part of the Ernest Meyer Collection of the Tebeau-Field Library of Florida History in Cocoa. Meyer's photographic record of this trip, captured on more than 300 glass negatives, provides an unusual look at the adventures of early Tin Canners. (Courtesy of the Ernest Meyer Collection, Tebeau-Field Library.)

The 1909 Tampa-Jacksonville Endurance Run was the first cross-state automobile journey in Florida. Drivers were forced to find their own roads and to map those that were suitable for automobiles. (Courtesy of the University of South Florida Library, Special Collections Department.)

One of the earliest advertisements aimed at Tin Can tourists was this 1915 postcard printed for St. Augustine's Post Cottage Camp, which offered cottages, rooms, and apartments in addition to house car, trailer, and tent spaces. The map provided directions to the tourist attractions in the Oldest City, along with information about shopping opportunities.

COMPLIMENTS OF
POST COTTAGE CAMP
ST. AUGUSTINE, FLA.   6 Dixie Highway, South
Established 1915   "Selected for Your Comfort"
Telephone and Telegraph Service.
LOCATION: IN THE CITY, on U. S.—1, or
Florida —- 4, going SOUTH from WEST KING
STREET, only 3 minutes' walk to Shopping
Center, 8 minutes' drive to Beaches.

Early auto camps were often little more than backyards or lawns that offered access to water and some security. This Meyer photograph spotlights the sparseness of the accommodations at such a camp south of Jacksonville in 1922. (Courtesy of the Ernest Meyer Collection, Tebeau-Field Library.)

The completion of the Dixie Highway from Montreal to Miami in 1915 was cause for celebration for these Brevard County residents. Anita Travis, Arlene Wooten, and Maude Hindle represent the points on the road, while members of the Dixie Highway Committee occupy the car. Seated in the front are Charlie Tarter and Ed Grimes. Bill Myers, Roy Packard, and Gus Thomas occupy the back seat.

Along the Road near Rockledge Hotel. Rockledge, Fl.

This stretch of road near Rockledge was considered an improved road for the early 1900s. Eventually this road, winding its way along the western shore of the Indian River Lagoon, would become part of U.S. Highway 1, a major north-south route for motorists. Taken in front of the Hiram Smith Williams House, this picture shows the artesian well that was initially maintained for horses and oxen teams. Tin Canners frequently stopped here to add water to boiling radiators and to replenish water containers.

Despite the sometimes-rough stretches of road, Tin Can tourists found the natural beauty of Florida hard to resist. Ernest Meyer photographed this tranquil scene of the bank of the New River at Fort Lauderdale. (Courtesy of the Ernest Meyer Collection, Tebeau-Field Library.)

13

Meyer took this picture of his wife, Jennie, on the beach at Fort Lauderdale. He lyrically entitled it, "What were the waves saying?" Although most of his photographs were shots of camps and campers, he occasionally indulged in more artistic themes. Jennie was a favorite subject of such pictures. (Courtesy of the Ernest Meyer Collection, Tebeau-Field Library.)

Because of the possibility of an outbreak of infectious diseases or the transmittal of agricultural pests, Florida maintained inspection stations at various points around the state. Persons and plants suspected of carrying diseases were quarantined until they were determined to be safe. Here, a National Guardsman stops traffic at an inspection station near Melbourne. (Courtesy of the Ernest Meyer Collection, Tebeau-Field Library.)

14

This small shed, photographed by Ernest Meyer in 1922, is the oldest schoolhouse in Brevard County. It is currently located on the campus of the Florida Institute of Technology in Melbourne. Notice the small bridge to the left, which carries the intriguing sign, "Tar Heel." None of the old-timers in the area can remember why the sign or the bridge were put there. (Courtesy of the Ernest Meyer Collection, Tebeau-Field Library.)

Early auto camps often consisted of little more than a cleared space on the side of a dirt road. Ernest Meyer took this picture of his camp at Royal Palm State Park near Florida City. Although the glass negative for this print has suffered some deterioration, the viewer can discern two African Americans standing with Meyer in front of his tent. (Courtesy of the Ernest Meyer Collection, Tebeau-Field Library.)

In this apparently staged group photograph at the Barnacle Club south of Melbourne on the Indian River, Meyer managed to captured the simplicity of life on the road. Even the dog seems posed on his wooden pedestal, while the cat on the top of the tent surveys the scene with apparent disdain. (Courtesy of the Ernest Meyer Collection, Tebeau-Field Library.)

When no restaurants or stores were nearby, Tin Canners often took advantage of Florida's streams and lakes to supplement their larders. This camper, identified only as "Ed," was so proud of his catch that he had the photograph made into a postcard to send to his friend. Writing to his sister-in-law, Mrs. Lee Wimmer of Asbury Park, New Jersey, he described his efforts, "Oh, Boy! This is me cooking, no, I mean frying, not right yet, I meant melting . . . ."

As they journeyed through the Sunshine State, Tin Canners took advantage of the many attractions that earlier tourists who came by boat or train enjoyed. One of the pre-Disney attractions that thrilled tourists was this gigantic live oak tree near Daytona Beach. More than 100 feet high, its trunk had a circumference of 36 feet while the canopy measured more than 160 feet.

Although some roads in Florida were fairly wide and well maintained, the torrential rains of the spring and summer could frequently inundate the best of them with several inches of water. Country roads were even more susceptible to washouts. This flooded creek near Valkaria in Brevard County covers the wooden bridge, and water floods its banks some 50 feet from its normal channel. (Courtesy of the Ernest Meyer Collection, Tebeau-Field Library.)

18

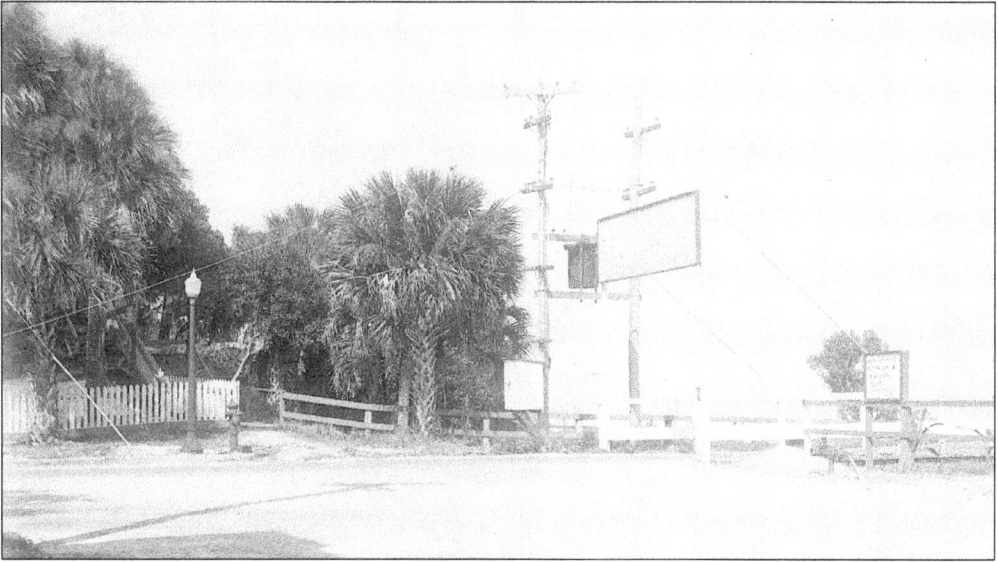

Early motorists frequently encountered roads that, while well known to local residents, presented a myriad of choices and few directional signs. This bridge between Melbourne and Indialantic, photographed in 1921, was well marked. The high bluff to the left of the picture was a favorite courting place for young couples in Melbourne. (Courtesy of the Ernest Meyer Collection, Tebeau-Field Library.)

DeSota [sic] Park in Tampa was the birthplace of the Tin Can Tourist Association. The park's name, which honored the Spanish explorer Hernando DeSoto, who landed in the Tampa Bay area in 1539, was usually misspelled. The early park amounted to little more than cleared areas among pine, palm, and oak trees. From 1919 until 1977, Tin Canners met twice a year (once in a Florida locale and once in a Michigan camp). (Courtesy of the Ernest Meyer Collection, Tebeau-Field Library.)

Easy Street was the main thoroughfare in Tampa's DeSota Park. Tin Canners could legitimately write home to family and friends that they were "in Florida and living on Easy Street." (Courtesy of the Ernest Meyer Collection, Tebeau-Field Library.)

Roadside "Mom-and-Pop" stores offered tourists the opportunity to stop and rest, while enjoying fresh citrus and local produce. In later years, Stuckey's and Horne's took the same basic concept and created nationwide businesses providing the same kinds of services on a highly commercial basis. (Courtesy of the Ernest Meyer Collection, Tebeau-Field Library.)

21

The Gainesville Tin Can Tourist Camp offered all of the amenities to the traveler. It also offered a close proximity to such attractions as Silver Springs, where Elizabeth Jaffery, in a 1925 letter to her mother, described how she had boarded one of the glass-bottomed boats "and looked 80 feet down in the water. It is impossible to describe it, it is so wonderful."

The Leon Hotel in Fort Myers, c. 1920, offered tourists accommodations "on the DIXIE Highway." Notice the extra tires strapped on the side of the auto at the extreme right. Interestingly, the Dixie Highway, which opened in 1915, ran from Montreal to Miami on the *east* coast of Florida, while Fort Myers is on the Gulf coast.

The St. Cloud Tourist Club House in rural St. Cloud had a shuffleboard club with more than 100 members. The message written on the back of this postcard to Edd M. Cutting of Lyme Center, New Hampshire, was a friendly taunt from his friend, "Win." "We read of snow, cold and deaths in the north. Nothing like that here. Am in my shirt sleeves everyday."

Daytona Beach provided its annual visitors an auditorium, shuffleboard courts, and a "headquarters" building.

Lantana is famous today as the center of tabloid journalism in the United States. In 1921, however, it was a favorite camping area for Tin Canners. Although accommodations were sparse, Tin Canners made do. The communal showers and restrooms provided a welcome respite after a day of travel or sightseeing. (Courtesy of the Ernest Meyer Collection, Tebeau-Field Library.)

The camp at West Palm Beach offered wide-open spaces where Tin Canners could set up for a single night or erect more permanent structures for longer stays. This 1921 Ernest Meyer photograph shows the wide variety of tents and shelters erected in the camp. (Courtesy of the Ernest Meyer Collection, Tebeau-Field Library.)

When Tin Canners saw something of interest, they simply pulled over to the side of the road and set up their camp. Such was the case when Ernest and Jennie Meyer spied the tile factory in the background. Their car, covered by a tarpaulin, is barely visible in the center of the picture. (Courtesy of the Ernest Meyer Collection, Tebeau-Field Library.)

The wide beach at West Palm Beach was made up of hard-packed sand. Tin Canners loved to camp on the sand and catch the refreshing breezes from the Atlantic Ocean. Jennie Meyer and the Meyer's traveling companion, "Cat," seem to be enjoying themselves. (Courtesy of the Ernest Meyer Collection, Tebeau-Field Library.)

Miami, the city that Henry Flagler put on the map, was a favorite destination for Tin Canners. They could find a variety of camps, ranging from the open spaces of this autopark to airy shelters (below) with open shutters, vented roofs, and screened doors. Notice the several boxes tied to the "running board" and rear of the car in the picture above. These boxes contained essential supplies, spare parts, and the amenities that made a camp homey. (Courtesy of the Ernest Meyer Collection, Tebeau-Field Library.)

The Zephyrhills Tourist Club (*c.* 1955) was not as plush as the facilities in Daytona Beach, but tourists could find information and entertainment here, including the omnipresent shuffleboard courts.

This trailer camp was neat and attractively landscaped. Many Tin Canners permanently located their trailers in small parks (notice the flowerbeds in front of the trailers) and simply drove their cars down to Florida during the winter months. This pattern still holds true today in such towns as Zephyrhills, Lutz, Melbourne, and hundreds of others.

Trailer Haven in Melbourne offered large 40-by-30-foot lots, a snack bar, store, and recreation hall for its patrons. Trailers with bathrooms were also allowed to tap into city sewage lines. Located near Highway 192, which ran to the central Florida town of Kissimmee, tourists could park their trailers here and have easy access to the Indian River, the Atlantic Ocean, or to the Central Florida highlands.

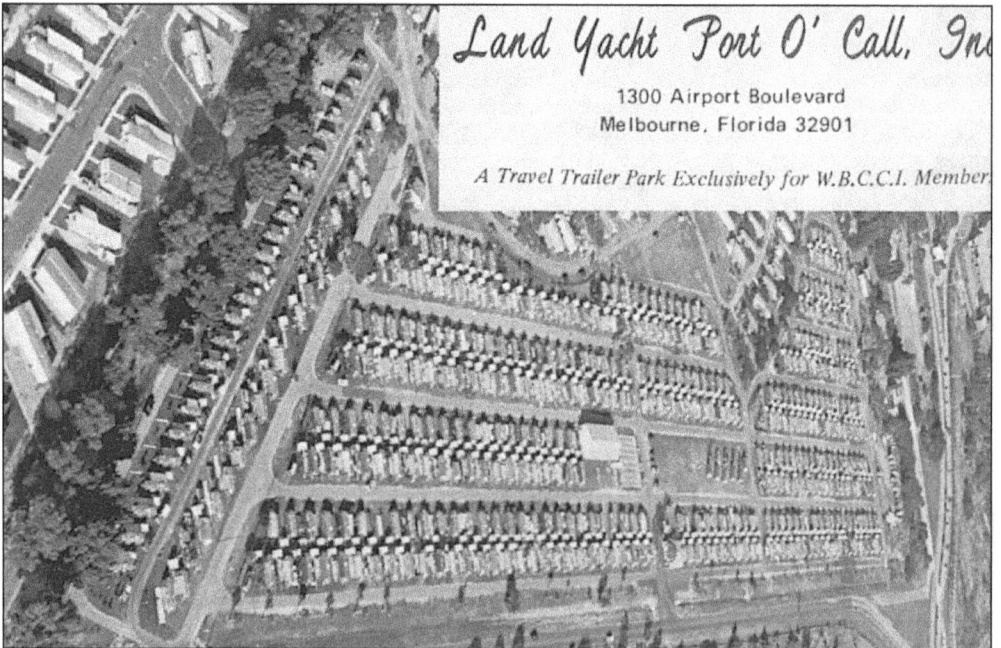

Land Yacht Port O' Call, Inc

1300 Airport Boulevard
Melbourne, Florida 32901

A Travel Trailer Park Exclusively for W.B.C.C.I. Members

By the early 1960s, some trailer parks had become specialized. This park near Melbourne catered to owners of the famous Airstream trailers, designed by Wally Byam, constructed of airplane aluminum and registered with specific serial numbers. The park is still in operation.

L.E. Browder operated the Bayside Tourist Park, built in 1940–1941, on Pensacola Bay. Tin Canners could park their own trailer on available slabs or stay in small cabins on the property. Water, electricity, and an on-site store provided all of the amenities. Visitors could take advantage of fishing, boating, and swimming. During World War II, such camps provided affordable housing for service wives who wanted to be near husbands training in nearby military facilities.

A Trailer Camp in Florida 189

This unidentified Florida trailer camp (c. 1938) shows a more temporary population. Streets are dirt, lots are unimproved, and communal showers and bathrooms are provided at the rear of the camp. Nevertheless, the postcard legend noted that "Hundreds of visitors yearly arrive in Florida aboard their 'home on wheels.' Some of the best equipped and certainly the most beautiful camps in the country are to be found in this Sunshine Land, planned exclusively for their use."

Bradenton Trailer Park, Bradenton, Florida—40

Notice the variety of trailer styles that can be found in the Bradenton Trailer Park in 1938. "A delightful haven for trailer tourists," goes the legend on the card. "Its shady park with facilities for comfort and its enjoyable location make a popular stop over."

This image shows the Bradenton Trailer Park in 1946. The description of the park declares that its 800 lots have "all the modern conveniences including electric meters, water piped to each trailer, paved street, etc." As an added draw, "Free programs are provided daily throughout the winter season."

B-13—Bradenton Trailer Park, Bradenton, Fla.

A third view of the Bradenton Trailer Park shows the park as it was in 1960. The Bradenton Kiwanis Club owned and operated the camp, and the profits made from its operation went to local charities. Over the years, the trailer park changed in appearance as more and more permanent residents added shelters, flower beds, and porches.

The patrons of Hickson Beauty Salon in Lebanon, Indiana, received this card from "Noble and Lola" in 1950. The Municipal Trailer Park in Punta Gorda was so close to the water that one could "walk out the trailer door and start to fish." Notice the varied styles of the trailers, which seldom exceeded 20 feet in length.

Trailer Square in Plant City had room for 204 trailers. The management provided a large recreation hall and two laundries. Residents could buy necessities at the shopping center across the street.

32

Some trailer parks, such as the Arrow Trailer Park on Highway 98 at Santa Rosa, Florida, were little more than open fields with little to no shelter against the intense Florida sunshine or the elements. The Arrow consisted of a mere 2.5 acres and also catered to the transient over-the-road drivers.

Tin Can tourists frequently stopped at small service stations to get gasoline and supplies. Although this is a replica of a 1920s station, its creator, Paul Holt, featured all of the services offered to the motoring public (tire repair, air, gasoline, kerosene, soft drinks, and even a postal drop box).

Tourist Cafe — Waukeenah, Fla.
Place of Rest

T.K. Victory was only one of the many cafe operators who catered to tourists. His "Tourist Cafe," located in Waukeenah (c. 1953), offered "Good food, prompt and courteous service."

All the major highways leading into Florida featured "mom and pop" citrus stands that offered the finest Florida fruit, novelties of all kinds, and assorted displays of exotic animals. This is the Snyder Citrus House in DeLand on Highway 17.

Even the busiest Tin Canners found it necessary to stop occasionally and do household chores such as washing clothes. This football goal post next to the autocamp at Bradenton proved extremely useful as a temporary clothesline. (Courtesy of the Ernest Meyer Collection, Tebeau-Field Library.)

The plentiful streams and lakes of Florida provided an easy way to supplement diets of tinned food. Ernest Meyer took this self-portrait with a string of catfish near Valkaria on the Indian River. (Courtesy of the Ernest Meyer Collection, Tebeau-Field Library.)

This tiny "community house" at the Leesburg tourist camp provided campers with a screened meeting place where they could meet and swap stories of their adventures on the road. (Courtesy of the Ernest Meyer Collection, Tebeau-Field Library.)

Early Tin Canners in Florida used cars of every description. From larger touring sedans to runabouts, the only requirement was that the automobile be reliable. Notice the unusual cooking stove at the rear of the car to the extreme left. Notice also the string of laundry tied to the tree at the extreme right of the photograph. (Courtesy of the Ernest Meyer Collection, Tebeau-Field Library.)

Seminole-styled "chickees," made of palm poles and fronds, provide Tin Canners with additional opportunities to spread out in this camp near West Palm Beach. Electricity was provided by the lines stretched on crudely cut and pruned pine trees. (Courtesy of the Ernest Meyer Collection, Tebeau-Field Library.)

An open space with a picnic table and fire pit was all that was needed to transform the side of the road into a temporary home for Tin Canners. Ernest and Jennie Meyer and "Cat" eat their noonday meal before setting off to explore the citrus packing shed and groves in the background. (Courtesy of the Ernest Meyer Collection, Tebeau-Field Library.)

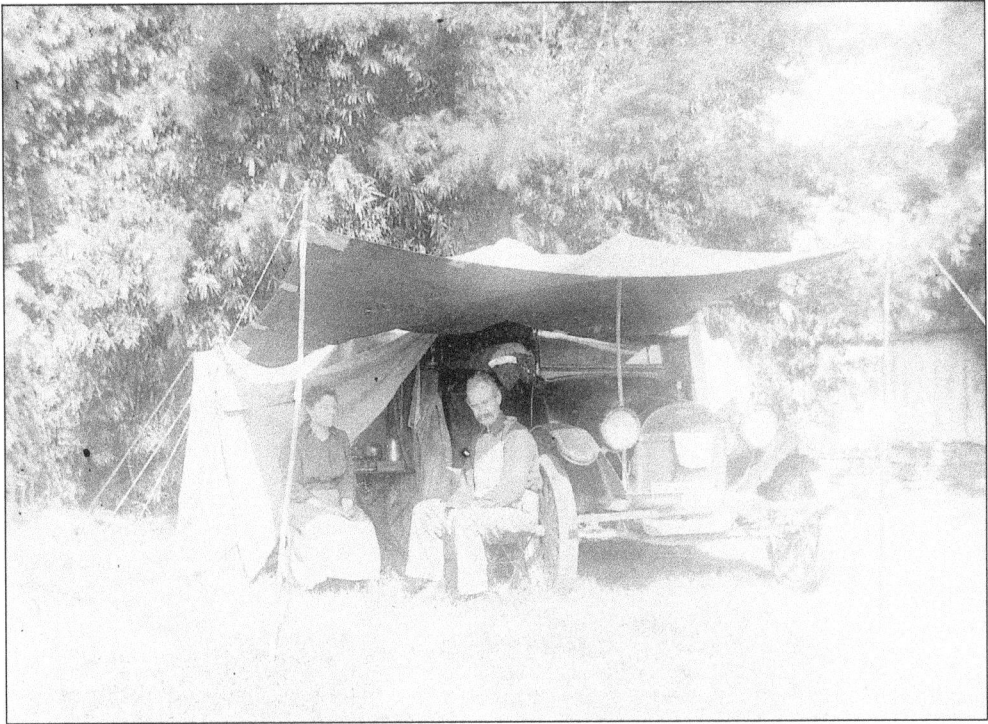

Ernest and Jenny Meyer were early visitors to Orlando, even before there was a Disney corporation. This bamboo grove provided an excellent place to set up camp. (Courtesy of the Ernest Meyer Collection, Tebeau-Field Library.)

From simple tarpaulins draped over an automobile to more substantial tents the size of small houses, Tin Canners used a variety of shelters on their meanderings through the Sunshine State. Ernest and Jenny Meyer enjoy the company of unknown neighbors in this 1922 photograph of a camp near Orlando. Notice the large American flag on the front windshield of the car on the right. (Courtesy of the Ernest Meyer Collection, Tebeau-Field Library.)

Automobiles and hard-packed sandy beaches are synonymous with Daytona today. In this 1922 picture by Ernest Meyer, the automobile also shared the same stretch of beach with a bi-plane. Jenny Meyer and an unknown man pose in from of the Meyer car. (Courtesy of the Ernest Meyer Collection, Tebeau-Field Library.)

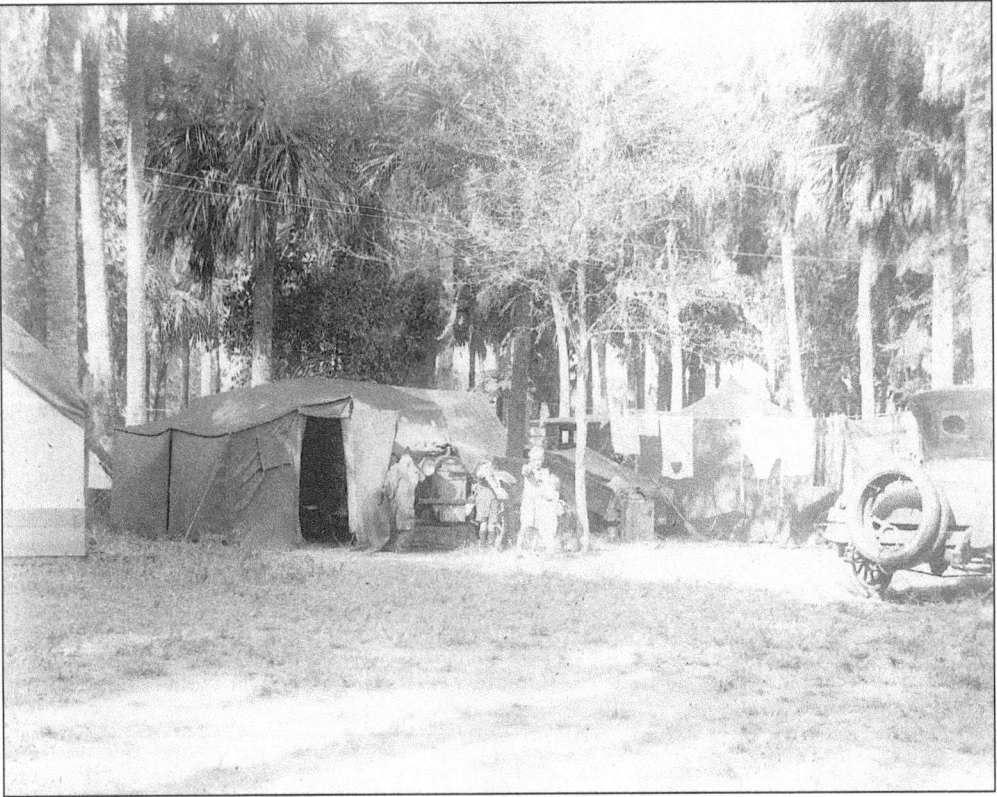

Anonymous children at the autocamp in Daytona play among the tents, hanging laundry, and parked automobiles. Notice the extra tires fastened to the rear of the auto at the extreme right of the photograph. (Courtesy of the Ernest Meyer Collection, Tebeau-Field Library.)

This portion of the Dixie Highway along the Halifax River south of Daytona was completed in 1922 and offered Tin Canners a paved surface and an up-close view of the river. (Courtesy of the Ernest Meyer Collection, Tebeau-Field Library.)

The autocamp at Ormond Beach offered parking space, semi-permanent tents that could be rented, and communal showers in 1922. (Courtesy of the Ernest Meyer Collection, Tebeau-Field Library.)

Ernest and Jenny Meyer appear to be the sole occupants of this autocamp near DeLand. Although separated by only 20 miles from the Ormond Beach camp, the DeLand camp offers much more in the way of shade and scenery. (Courtesy of the Ernest Meyer Collection, Tebeau-Field Library.)

The gentle waves of the Gulf of Mexico did not pack the beach sand as hard as the roaring Atlantic Ocean, but Jenny Meyer and "Cat" find it just as pleasant. (Courtesy of the Ernest Meyer Collection, Tebeau-Field Library.)

In 1922, Hobe Sound was little more than a barren landscape on the Indian River. Today, it is home to the very rich who make their winter homes in the Sunshine State. The tops of the trees in the background provide a good guide to the topography of the area. Florida's east coast is just a few feet above sea level, and each year, the Atlantic Ocean claims more and more of the land through erosion. (Courtesy of the Ernest Meyer Collection, Tebeau-Field Library.)

This Ernest Meyer photograph of the Withlacoochee River near Brooksville captures the splendid beauty of Florida's wilderness. A solitary fisherman is barely visible in the center of the photograph, while the outlines of farm buildings are in the treeline to the left. The paradox of such isolated beauty in close proximity to developed land is still a feature of the Florida landscape. (Courtesy of the Ernest Meyer Collection, Tebeau-Field Library.)

The sponge docks at Tarpon Springs proved as quaintly picturesque to Ernest Meyer in 1922 as they do to visitors today. Tarpon Springs was settled by Greeks and, until the mid-1940s, was a center for the sponge industry in the United States. A devastating epidemic among sponges and the development of artificial sponges severely crippled this industry. (Courtesy of the Ernest Meyer Collection, Tebeau-Field Library.)

Automobiles line the dock in Tarpon Springs in 1922. Many of the sponge buyers drove to the docks to buy sponges directly from the divers. Today, the sponge industry has largely disappeared, and the docks cater more to sightseers than to working divers. (Courtesy of the Ernest Meyer Collection, Tebeau-Field Library.)

This Ernest Meyer photograph offers a wonderful montage of different elements of Florida tourism in 1922. In the foreground, the configuration of the automobile shows how Tin Canners traveled, while the clothing of Ernest and Jenny Meyer shows how formally tourists dressed while sightseeing, and the cluster of Tarpon Springs sponge boats in the background provides a clue as to the kinds of things Tin Canners were interested in. (Courtesy of the Ernest Meyer Collection, Tebeau-Field Library.)

The glass negatives in the Ernest Meyer Collection of the Tebeau-Field Library contain rare images of landmarks long disappeared. This is the famous shell mound south of Daytona. The shells were deposited by early Native Americans, whose diet consisted mostly of shellfish. (Courtesy of the Ernest Meyer Collection, Tebeau-Field Library.)

The Daytona shell mound was the highest physical feature along the Mosquito Inlet coast, and early European navigators used it as a guide to steer a straight course. This mound and others along the coast provided the foundations for earliest improved roads in the vicinity. (Courtesy of the Ernest Meyer Collection, Tebeau-Field Library.)

Jenny Meyer, like other Tin Canners who would follow, was intrigued by the banana trees that grew in semi-tropical Florida. This cluster near Titusville rose more than 15 feet in the air. (Courtesy of the Ernest Meyer Collection, Tebeau-Field Library.)

The flat Florida pine scrubland, home to wandering herds of free-range cattle, provided an interesting subject for Meyer's camera. This scrubland near Valkaria was used by several families who gathered their cattle annually and sorted them out. (Courtesy of the Ernest Meyer Collection, Tebeau-Field Library.)

48

Early Tin Can tourist camps differed very little in their layout or the amenities offered. While the photographs collected here are very similar in composition, they are the earliest known images of these camps and are extremely rare. This is the camp in Ft. Pierce on the Atlantic coast. (Courtesy of the Ernest Meyer Collection, Tebeau-Field Library.)

The autocamp in Clearwater (above) closely resembled the one in St. Petersburg (below).
(Courtesy of the Ernest Meyer Collection, Tebeau-Field Library.)

Wooden crates and homemade chairs provide a semblance of outdoor comfort for these Tin Canners in the Dunellon autocamp. (Courtesy of the Ernest Meyer Collection, Tebeau-Field Library.)

Small cabins at the Lake Okeechobee autocamp offered Tin Canners the opportunity to take a break from tenting and stretch out on a full-size bed. Cabin rents were nominal and offered a change from continuous camping. Notice the community toilets at the extreme left edge of this picture. (Courtesy of the Ernest Meyer Collection, Tebeau-Field Library.)

This makeshift table provided the Meyers an opportunity to lunch in style in the "jungle" of Royal Palm State Park south of Florida City. (Courtesy of the Ernest Meyer Collection, Tebeau-Field Library.)

Surplus military tents were favorites of Tin Canners who enjoyed the tents' spaciousness, ease of movement, and resistance to the elements. This camp in Stuart shows some of the ways Tin Canners used these tents. Notice the covered truck behind the tents at the left of the picture. Tin Canners quickly adapted every kind of vehicle for use on the road. (Courtesy of the Ernest Meyer Collection, Tebeau-Field Library.)

The fishing wharf at Vero Beach offered a quaint and artistic composition for the lens of Ernest Meyer. (Courtesy of the Ernest Meyer Collection, Tebeau-Field Library.)

This primitive fishing camp near Sebastian on the Indian River provided an interesting contrast in the evolution of buildings in Florida. The log cabin on the right was typical of the kinds of structures erected by the area's earliest settlers, while the "lean to" in the center is made of sawed lumber. The two men on the left side are holding a large fish caught nearby. (Courtesy of the Ernest Meyer Collection, Tebeau-Field Library.)

Although disfigured by time and fading, this 1924 Meyer print is the first in a series of three remarkable pictures of a community barbecue at the Arcadia autocamp. (Courtesy of the Ernest Meyer Collection, Tebeau-Field Library.)

Tin Canners hired African-American workers to dig a large pit for the barbecue. Two smaller pits, filled with coals from fires that burned all night, are spaced on either side of the larger pit. This was to prevent the spread of cooking fires into the nearby woods. Large portions of pork and beef were then cooked on the open pits. (Courtesy of the Ernest Meyer Collection, Tebeau-Field Library.)

Once the meat was cooked, it was taken to tables under a canvas shelter and carefully rendered into smaller, more easily managed portions. (Courtesy of the Ernest Meyer Collection, Tebeau-Field Library.)

By 1925, auto-tourism was beginning to take on a different face. Instead of tents, Tin Canners now pulled small trailers behind their cars or made arrangements to stay in small cabins or motels along the way. This 1924 picture of a pine lane north of Stuart is an appropriate ending for this chapter on early Tin Canners. (Courtesy of the Ernest Meyer Collection, Tebeau-Field Library.)

Two

TIN CAN TOURISTS
THE SECOND AND THIRD WAVES

Although the original Tin Can tourists carried tents with them, the rough life of camping quickly gave way to more permanent trailer parks and tourists "homes." By 1925, the large number of annual visitors demanded more and more comfortable lodgings, and while some pulled these lodgings with them as "house trailers," others took advantage of local lodgings. Throughout Florida, hundreds of large family homes were converted to tourist facilities, where rooms could be rented by the day, week, month, or for several months at a time.

In some areas, tourists from northern states maintained their home state identity by camping or renting in the same area. In such out-of-the-way places as Titusville, Arcadia, Punta Gorda, or Okeechobee, it was not unusual to find Tin Canners celebrating "Michigan Day" or "Ohio Day" with communal picnics and festivals.

In addition to the conversion of private homes, many small motels or "motor hotels" sprang up. The first of these were little more than small cabins offering sleeping accommodations, but gradually they offered kitchenettes, pools, and, after World War II, air conditioning. Many Tin Canners found accommodations they liked and could afford for an extended period and returned year after year. Operators became familiar with their regular visitors and considered them more as family than customers. It was not unusual for owner-operators to maintain a steady correspondence with their patrons during the off-season.

During World War II, these small motels provided the families of servicemen places to stay near their husbands, fathers, sons, and boyfriends. More than two million servicemen were stationed in the Sunshine State during the war, and when the war ended, they returned with their families for vacations. Often they returned to the same areas where they received their training.

McRorie's Tourist Home in Jacksonville offered tourists "Good beds, good eats, clean linens for only $1.00 a day." Private baths pushed the price up to $1.50. McRorie's was typical of the thousands of such establishments that accommodated tourists in towns and cities throughout the nation.

Promoters of Florida's land boom in the early 1920s mailed millions of postcards to Tin Canners in an effort to attract them to new towns and developments. The Crystal Beach Development Company in St. Petersburg mailed this card in 1924 to tout its development. The company promised an additional five free postcards "if you ask for them."

58

Ernest and Jenny Meyer found this arch on the Tamiami Trail, which stretched from Tampa to Miami, at the Collier County line. Collier County was created in 1923 and named in honor of Barron G. Collier, who developed Naples and the surrounding area. This sign was newly erected. (Courtesy of the Ernest Meyer Collection, Tebeau-Field Library.)

Miss M.E. Williams of Melbourne operated the "Ohio Guest House," which catered to tourists from that state.

As more and more visitors made the trek to Florida by automobile, small motels opened to provide lodgings for a night or a month. Many tourists found it easier to simply pack their belongings and kids in the car and take advantage of these cheap motels. This is the Rex Motel at 2939 Hillsborough Avenue in Tampa. Potential customers were assured that the motel was "state inspected" and featured excellent drinking water, innerspring mattresses, kitchenettes, and hot and cold water in every cabin.

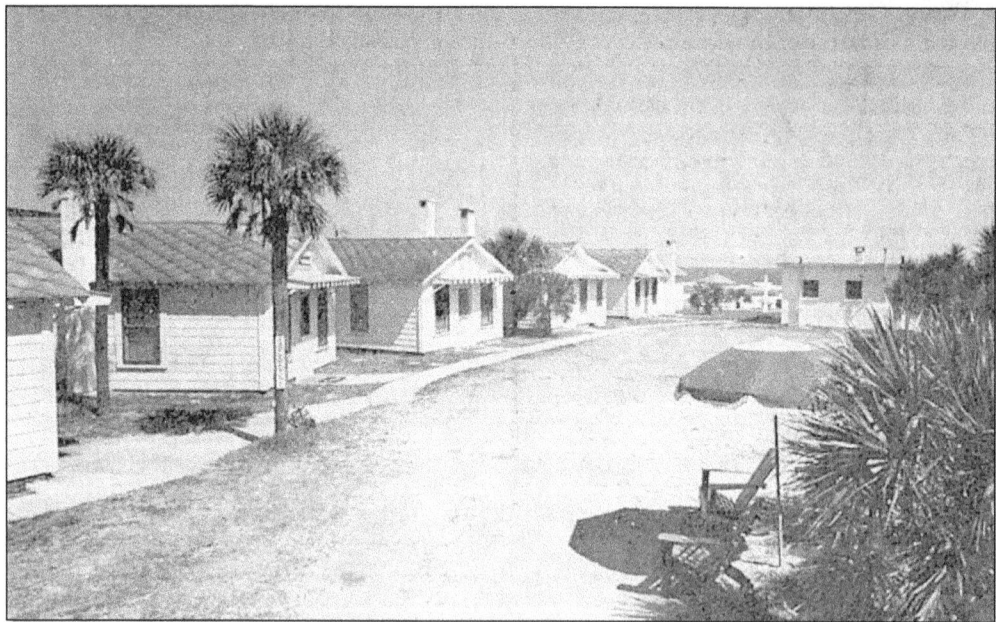

R.P. Smith, the owner and operator of Beach Haven Cottages on South Atlantic Avenue in Daytona Beach, advertised his motel as "A nice place for nice people." Many first-time visitors were so pleased with the family atmosphere of some of these small motels that they returned year after year.

There was a "sameness" to the small motel operations in Florida. This is the Cactus Terrace in Key West, which offered individual cabins with private showers, hot water, recreation facilities, and "shade." It was, according to its operator, the best place "for a pleasant stay in the southernmost city."

The Cocoa Cottages, located on Highway 1, were owned by H.B. Berdan and managed by Frank Landsdowne. The cottages featured private baths and open fireplaces for heat. Conveniently located "mid-way between Jacksonville and Miami," tourists could take advantage of the Atlantic beaches, which were just a few miles away, or the fishing on the Indian River.

The Indianola Hotel Court, owned and operated by Van C. Wesley and later by Ted Buri, was located in Eau Gallie on the "Holiday Highway," one of the many names given to U.S. Highway 1. Although the Indianola Hotel Court did offer modern guestrooms with private baths, it was awfully short on shade trees.

Mr. and Mrs. W.A. Lethio were the owners and operators of Christine's Travel Court in Eau Gallie. By the early 1950s, this motel offered its guests telephones in each room and the assurance of being approved by the AAA.

Highland Hotel Court U. S. 1

Melbourne, Fla.

Owner James H. Pruitt claimed his Highland Hotel Court was located on the highest point on the Indian River, some two miles north of Melbourne. In addition to the 25 steam-heated cottages, guests could take advantage of the nearby beaches, golf courses, and salt water or fresh water fishing. They could find anything they needed at the restaurants, garages, grocery stores, and service stations in the area.

The Palm Bay Tourist Camp was located on Orange Avenue in Palm Bay. The camp had 40 cottages located on the shores of the Indian River, where guests could find the finest fishing in Florida.

Highway 1 was the major north-south route for the east coast of Florida. Small motels and tourist camps lined the roads at every major crossroads or town. Many, such as the Palm Terrace Court, south of Melbourne, are still in existence. Their days as clean, reliable, and reputable places to stay are long over, and they function more as housing for transient workers or the very poor.

The River Oak Cabin Park was typical of the small motels that were found along the major highways of Florida. The River Oak's office was located in the small octagonal building in the center of the driveway. Individual cabins featured tiled showers and garages.

The Midway Tourist Colony in Melbourne presented a neat and tidy appearance. The wide streets and small cabins were kept in good order. This view shows Wall Street, the major street in the camp.

This is another view of the Midway Tourist Colony in Melbourne. These cabins were much larger than the ones on Wall Street and contained two bedrooms, a living room, bath, kitchen, and screened porch.

By the late 1950s and early 1960s, more modern hotel facilities were a staple of American highways. Gradually more and more amenities were offered. The Wayside Motel in Pensacola, operated by the Lawrence Heberts, offered air conditioning and television in each room to 1950s travelers.

Cocoa Shores, P. O. Box 85
Cocoa Beach, Florida

In the pre-condominium 1960s, visitors could rent spacious four- or five-room apartments, such as the Cocoa Shores, on the beach. Beach frontage is so valuable today that many of these smaller operations have been forced to close and sell to developers. The earliest memories of Florida for millions of Americans came from family vacations in similar places.

Casa Loma Lodge

ON U. S. 441, ½ MILE SOUTH OF GAINESVILLE, FLA.

Despite the competition by large chains, many small motels, like the Casa Loma Lodge south of Gainesville, still offer clean rooms at affordable prices for the thousands of new tourists who make their first trek to the Sunshine State. Vacations, long a privilege of the middle-to-upper classes in the United States, are now affordable for everyone. While the more wealthy might fly to Florida and stay at resorts, they have been replaced by a new class of traveling public that still enjoys the attractions of a few decades ago.

67

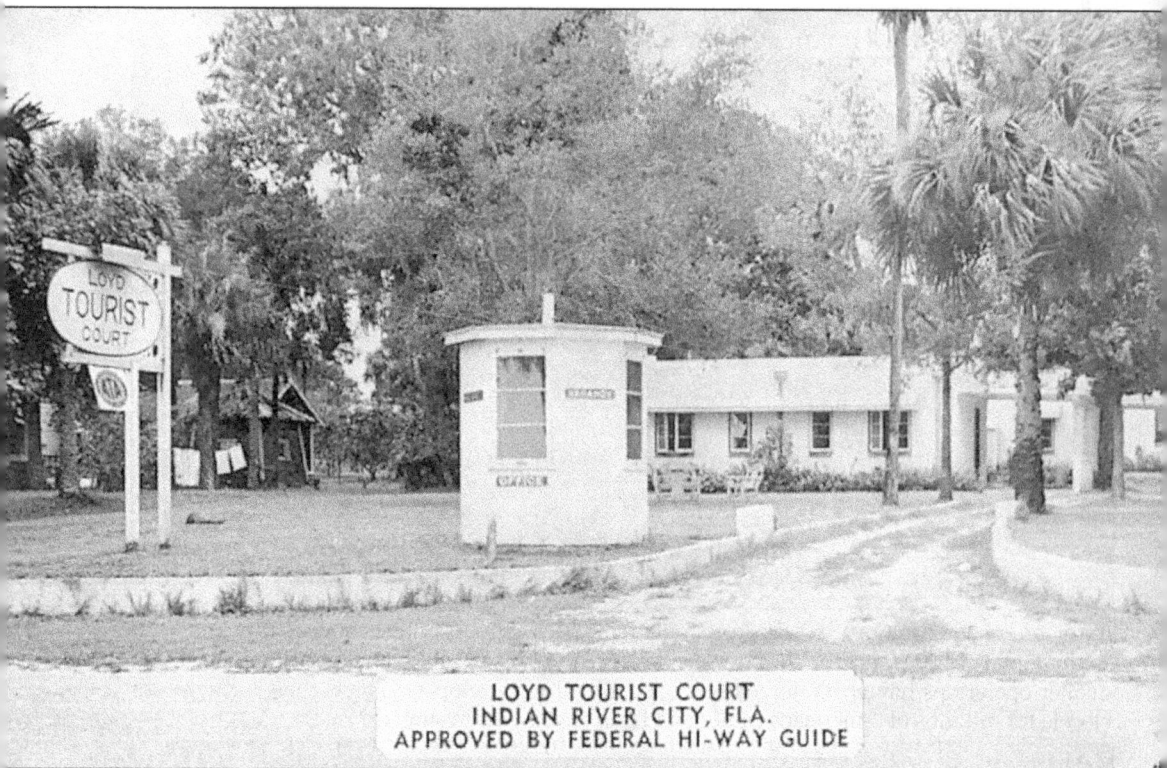

LOYD TOURIST COURT
INDIAN RIVER CITY, FLA.
APPROVED BY FEDERAL HI-WAY GUIDE

Mr. and Mrs. A.W. Loyd, owners and operators of the Loyd Tourist Court in Indian River City, four miles south of Titusville, offered their guests carpeted floors, all the modern conveniences, and great fishing in the Indian River from the court's own dock.

Three

VISIONS OF FLORIDA

1900–1930

Although Florida had gained a modest reputation as a center for tourism as early as the 1870s, the advent of automobile tourism during the first decade of the 20th century produced a tremendous increase in the number of visitors to the Sunshine State. The Tin Canners were a new breed of tourists, no longer bound by the static routes of railroads or steamboats, but free to make their own way throughout the state. No area was excluded from the inquisitive forays of these modern explorers. The earliest Tin Canners were intrigued by the wild beauty of this largely unexplored state, and its natural attractions drew their attention. Gradually, however, those who returned year after year wanted to see much more.

Throughout the state, permanent residents of the Sunshine State created an almost infinite variety of attractions, which, although lacking the polish of today's Disney or Universal Studios, still became favorites of the annual visitors. Drawing heavily on the natural fauna of the state, many of these attractions featured alligators, snakes, and deer. Still others, such as Silver Springs, were built around another of Florida's wonders—its water. The wild and untamed Everglades and the Native American inhabitants, the Seminoles, were curiosities waiting to be explored.

Rock outcroppings are so rare in the Sunshine State that an isolated coquina quarry near Titusville provided an unusual backdrop for this Ernest Meyer photograph. Coquina is a soft, porous rock formed from millions of tiny shells from an assortment of sea creatures. Jennie Meyer is dwarfed by the outcroppings. (Courtesy of the Ernest Meyer Collection, Tebeau-Field Library.)

This oak hammock near Wimauma, with its Spanish moss draped from every tree branch, provided tourists with a look at what Florida had been prior to European settlement. (Courtesy of the Ernest Meyer Collection, Tebeau-Field Library.)

Many of the attractions that had once entertained more affluent tourists of the late 19th century found new life with the influx of Tin Can tourists of the 20th century. This alligator farm near Jacksonville offered adventuresome children rides on a wagon pulled by a cooperative reptilian.

FOUNTAIN OF YOUTH. 1513.

St. Augustine's famous "Fountain of Youth" attracted a constant stream of Tin Canners. The "Oldest City" quickly created a wide assortment of other sights to lure the annual visitors to the area.

Old Joe, an alligator approximately 15 feet long, always drew tourists to his pen in Port Orange in Volusia County.

Tin Canners who visited West Palm Beach were fascinated by the local aquarium's alligator pond stocked with reptiles of all sizes and descriptions. Ernest Meyer captured this popular attraction in a series of pictures. (Courtesy of the Ernest Meyer Collection, Tebeau-Field Library.)

72

This is another view of the West Palm Beach alligator pond by Ernest Meyer in 1921. By the mid-1930s, practically every small roadside attraction or citrus stand featured a collection of these creatures. (Courtesy of the Ernest Meyer Collection, Tebeau-Field Library.)

Pelican Island, near Wabasso in the Indian River, was the first federally created bird sanctuary in the United States. President Theodore Roosevelt, at the urging of concerned citizens of the area, designated this island as a refuge for the brown pelican in 1906. (Courtesy of the Ernest Meyer Collection, Tebeau-Field Library.)

Ernest Meyer focused his camera on a group of pelicans on Pelican Island in 1922. Thousands of birds filled the air during the day, and one local resident described them as "so plentiful they blocked out the sun." A game warden prevented tourists from disturbing the birds, but no one could quench their curiosity about seeing them. (Courtesy of the Ernest Meyer Collection, Tebeau-Field Library.)

Any journey through the Everglades was a search for alligators, wild animals, and Seminole Indians, a small tribe driven to seek safety in the Everglades in the 1850s. The advent of automobile tourism resulted in the creation of villages near highways where Seminoles could be seen and photographed for a price of course. Seminoles became experts in providing the kinds of attractions, such as alligator wrestling, that brought tourists and tourist dollars to a people out of the mainstream of Florida's economy. (Courtesy of the Ernest Meyer Collection, Tebeau-Field Library.)

The natural beauty of Florida's swamps proved to be a strong lure for Tin Canners, who wanted to experience this last outpost of "wilderness" in North America. Ernest Meyer captured the haunting beauty of this slough in 1922. (Courtesy of the Ernest Meyer Collection, Tebeau-Field Library.)

For "Yankees," the presence of such exotic plants as the coconut tree gave Florida the appearance of a tropical paradise. Jenny Meyer, accompanied by an inquisitive neighborhood pooch, poses in front of these trees at the entrance to the Miami Causeway. (Courtesy of the Ernest Meyer Collection, Tebeau-Field Library.)

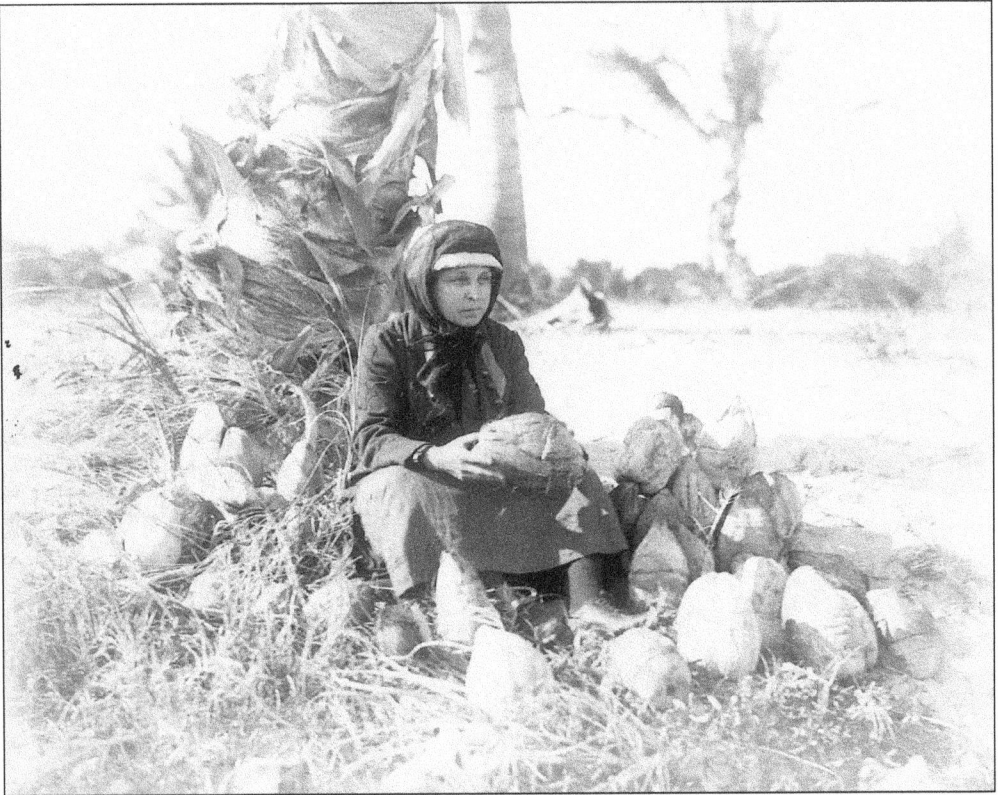

Jenny Meyer surrounded herself with coconuts for this typical tourist picture. (Courtesy of the Ernest Meyer Collection, Tebeau-Field Library.)

Few Tin Canners could pass up the quaint assemblage of fish houses on the Grant dock. From here, scores of fishermen would take their small boats into the Indian River Lagoon. Tourists enjoyed passing the time with local fisherman while fishing from the docks. (Courtesy of the Ernest Meyer Collection, Tebeau-Field Library.)

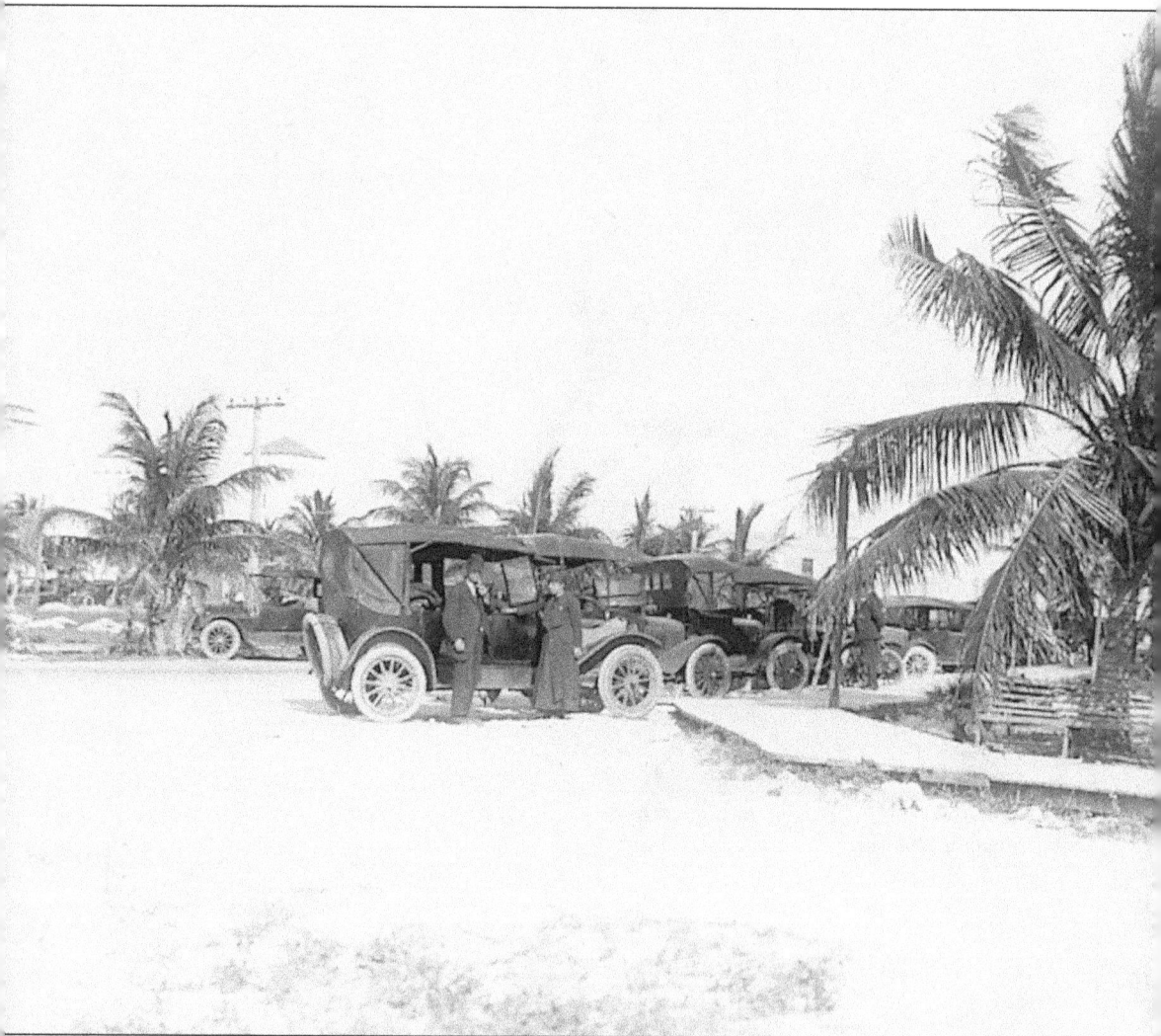

Tourists and local residents enjoyed visiting Florida's beaches. Unlike today's visitors, beachgoers in the early 20th century frequently ventured to the beach in business suits and ties. This Ernest Meyer photograph captures the scene at Miami Beach perfectly. (Courtesy of the Ernest Meyer Collection, Tebeau-Field Library.)

Feeding Deer on Carmichael Farm on Silver River.

One of the favorite spots for Tin Canners was Silver Springs. This postcard described the site as "unsurpassed in the World in grandeur and weird enchantment." Two young ladies feed the deer at Carmichael Farm near Silver Springs.

This is another view of tourists feeding deer at Carmichael Farm. Tin Canners mailed postcards like this to the "folks back home." The unusual flowers, Spanish moss, and exotic trees conveyed the message that the Sunshine State was a veritable Eden.

SHOWING VISITORS DEER, ON CARMICHAEL FARM ON SILVER RIVER.

Silver Springs offered swimmers a great opportunity to swim in the beautiful natural springs. Few swimmers can be found, however, in this 1920s view of the springs.

High divers draw attention from the crowd at Ponce de Leon Springs in 1927.

The Chatauqua at DeFuniak Springs enjoyed a brief revival during the early 1900s when Tin Canners discovered this quaint area of the Florida Panhandle.

When not visiting tourist attractions, many Tin Canners amused themselves by participating in a variety of activities such as competing in horseshoe pitching. This Lake Worth facility was dedicated solely to horseshoe pitching. Notice the large faux horseshoe on the clubhouse wall.

Excursion boats, *Mauretania* and *Lusitania*, offered pre-World War I tourists a view of Miami from Biscayne Bay.

Many municipalities sought to attract Tin Canners to their city by providing playing fields for sports and picnics. In this 1922 picture by Tampa's Burgert Brothers Studio, a large crowd of Tin Canners gather to watch some intense horseshoe competition.

Green Cove Springs, located on the banks of the St. Johns River, offered tourists and local residents an opportunity to meet and mingle at its casino. Early Tin Canners avidly sought out such local attractions on their jaunts through the Sunshine State.

Golf became an activity associated with the Sunshine State, and many Tin Canners took advantage of the large number of courses in Florida. Many cities provided public courses in order to attract Tin Canners and to satisfy the demands by local residents. This golfer tees off on the Fort Lauderdale Municipal Golf Links.

This *c.* 1930 image shows that the City of DeLand provided the "City Country Club," a miniature golf course for its tourists and residents. (Courtesy of the DeLand Photo Company.)

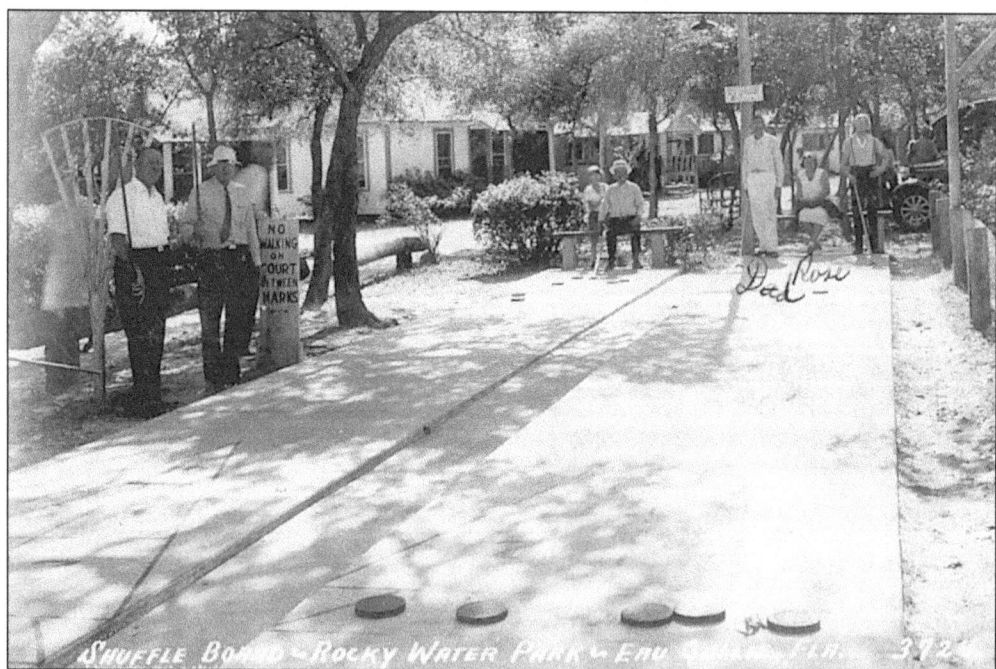

Like golf, shuffleboard became a sport that Tin Canners enjoyed between their travels along Florida's highways. Some cities maintained shuffleboard courts year round, and competitive leagues pitted city against city, trailer park against trailer park, and individual against individual. This is the court at Rocky Water Park in Eau Gallie.

Shuffleboard proved to be such an attraction to tourists that some towns held annual tournaments to decide local championships.

Tin Canners loved to send pictures like this one home to the folks up north. This is the swimming pool at Rocky Water Camp in Eau Gallie on Christmas Day, 1926. Such scenes captured the imagination of snow-bound Yankees and accounted for the steady annual increase in the number of tourists each year.

Just about every section of the Sunshine State had unusual natural features that attracted the attention of Tin Canners. This giant banyan tree near Fort Lauderdale was a favorite destination of many tourists.

While Fort Lauderdale claimed a giant banyan tree, tourists were also impressed with this giant cypress tree near Orlando. This tree stood more than 127 feet high, had a circumference of more than 47 feet, and a diameter of 17.5 feet.

The mysterious Seminoles, with their colorful clothes and history of warfare with the United States, provided Tin Canners with what they thought was a view of ancient Florida. Like the Tin Canners, the Seminoles were recent arrivals to Florida and traced their origins to the Lower Creeks of Georgia and Alabama.

Each year, young Greek sponge divers competed to retrieve the wooden cross thrown into Tarpon Springs by the local Greek Orthodox patriarch. This annual event was part of the ritual blessing of the fleet conducted by the Church. The lad who was successful in finding the cross and bringing it to the surface was supposed to enjoy good luck for the next year. Although the sponge industry has died out, this ritual is still conducted each year and draws thousands of tourists.

Greek Orthodox priests lead the annual Epiphany Day parade in Tarpon Springs. The parade was the prelude to the blessing of the fleet and the dive for the cross.

Eager young lads anxiously await the moment when the patriarch of the local Greek Orthodox Church will fling the cross into the water.

The beautifully manicured grounds of the former Tampa Bay Hotel drew hundreds of daily visitors. This is the famous "DeSoto Oak," the legendary site of Hernando DeSoto's headquarters in the Tampa Bay area.

This postcard, c. 1925, catches the mood of the Florida tourist industry. People came to the Sunshine State by automobile, by ship, and by dirigible. Although the number of dirigible passengers was negligible, this picture could also reflect the three major means of visiting Florida in the 20th and 21st centuries IF the dirigible was replaced with an airplane.

Four

THE YEAR-ROUND
PLAYGROUND

1930–1970

By the early 1920s, Florida had gained a reputation as a permanent year-round playground for tourists of all kinds. That reputation continued to grow during the 1930s and 1940s. World War II saw the establishment of hundreds of military bases in the Sunshine State, ranging from massive training camps at Camp Blanding (near Jacksonville) to small, out-of-the-way fighter bases in small towns and villages. More than two million men and women in all branches of service received their training in Florida. War industries also brought hundreds of thousands of men and women to the state. For some, duty or work in Florida was a return to a state with pleasant memories; for others, Florida was a vast unexplored playground.

Regardless of the reasons why people came to Florida, they were interested in seeing all there was to see. Because of the size of the state and the lack of public transportation, it was necessary to use automobiles to go from one tourist attraction to another. Despite gasoline rationing and some travel restrictions, GIs became tourists, seeking the same kinds of attractions that had entertained tourists for more than a century. Florida made such a positive impression on these temporary residents that many of them returned to the state as permanent residents when the war was over or as annual visitors. Between 1940 and 1960, the number of annual visitors to Florida grew from 2.25 million per year to 10.5 million. Tourism became the greatest single industry in the state, a position it still enjoys today.

L.C. Shadrick and Son were the proprietors of the "State Line Bar," which was located on U.S. Highway 41. Shadrick marketed his establishment as the "first-last" bar. That is to say, the last bar in Florida and the first bar in Georgia if you were traveling north, and vice versa if you were traveling south.

Just about every road leading into the Sunshine State between 1940 and 1965 was lined with small tourist stores offering a variety of animal life in small zoos, knickknacks, and cheap towels and chenille bedspreads. This ostrich farm near Jacksonville was one of the first tourist attractions visitors found when they entered the state.

Feeding the Black Bass at Silver Springs, Florida

Silver Springs remained a major tourist attraction until the mid-1970s. Although it still attracts a large number of visitors each year, it cannot compete with the larger theme parks in Orlando and Tampa.

These 1930s visitors enjoyed the same glass-bottomed boats at Silver Springs that a generation earlier had enjoyed while bathers frolicked in the springs. The proprietors promised that the water never exceeded a constant 72 degrees year round.

Weekiwachee Spring, located on Florida's west coast, offered tourists the unusual sight of living mermaids cavorting underwater. The spring became a favorite location for movie makers and movie stars, including Esther Williams.

O. 12— Sanlando Springs,
Tropical Park,
Orlando, Fla.

Water has always been intrinsic in Florida's attraction for tourists. In this 1940s photograph, bathers enjoy a summery afternoon swimming in Sanlando Springs near Orlando.

M-1—Top Deck at Marine Studios' Feeding Time,
Marineland, Fla.

The rapid growth of tourism resulted in the creation of new tourist attractions in Florida. Marineland, which opened on June 23, 1938, combined scientific research with daily shows that entertained visitors. Marineland recently closed its doors after 61 years because the changing patterns of tourism no longer brought enough visitors to support the facility.

K-2 SHUFFLE BOARD COURT, KISSIMMEE, FLORIDA

This 1948 postcard promoted the shuffleboard courts available to tourists in Kissimmee. Today Kissimmee is little more than small amusement parks, moderately priced motels, and strip mall after strip mall filled with tee-shirt shops. Its proximity to Disney World in Orlando has completely changed the economy of this small town.

WHAT Florida CITY AM I IN?

CLUE NO. 1: FAMED AS A CENTER OF THE ORANGE INDUSTRY, THIS IS FLORIDA'S LARGEST INLAND CITY

CLUE NO. 2: KNOWN AS FLORIDA'S "CITY BEAUTIFUL" WITH MORE THAN 30 LAKES WITHIN ITS CITY LIMITS.

LOVELY!

MISS 1ST PRIZE

I'M WAITING FOR YOU!

CLUE NO. 3: AROUND THIS CITY ARE THE FINEST FRESH WATER FISHING GROUNDS IN THE ENTIRE COUNTRY

ANSWER: ORLANDO

This early 1950s postcard promoted the attractions of Orlando. The emphasis on fishing, lakes, and oranges would change to Mickey Mouse, Donald Duck, and the Magic Kingdom just a decade later.

Florida's beaches have always attracted tourists. This is Miami Beach in 1947 before it became the home of fashion and entertainment personalities.

The boardwalk at Tower Beach in Fort Walton was a popular place for annual visitors and local residents. Florida's Gulf beaches were so popular with residents of Georgia, Alabama, and South Carolina that this stretch was (and still is) referred to as the "Redneck Riviera."

One of the premier tourist attractions for Tin Canners in Lake Wales was the Edward W. Bok Singing Tower and Bird Sanctuary, which was dedicated by Governor Doyle E. Carlton and President and Mrs. Calvin Coolidge in 1929. The Bok Tower still draws thousands of visitors each year but, like other earlier attractions, cannot compete with the modern theme parks.

Within a few years, Bok Tower became a major stop for the hundreds of excursion buses that served the tourist population. For the many Tin Canners who put this on their "must see" agenda, the nearby town of Lake Wales provided municipal camping facilities.

Visitors to Bok Tower could view this stone mosaic reproduction of DaVinci's *The Last Supper*. In addition, the tower carillon serenaded visitors hourly. It is difficult to imagine such an attraction drawing many visitors today.

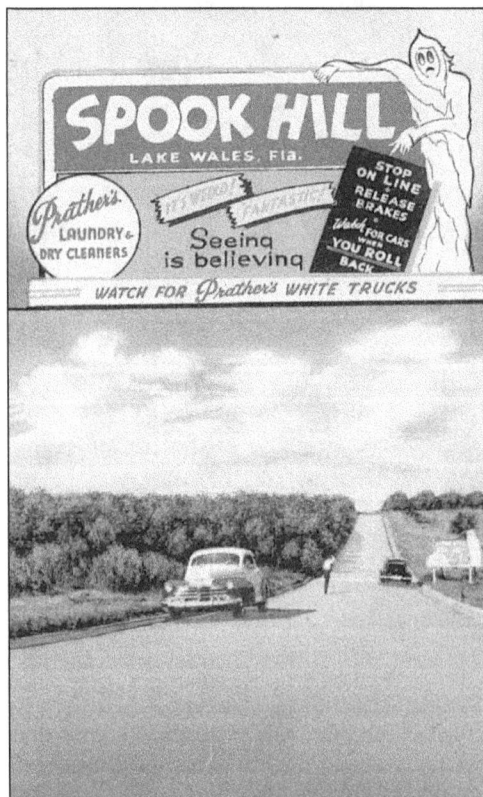

Lake Wales also featured the optical illusion of "Spook Hill," where "playful ghosts seize your car and . . . roll your vehicle gently backward uphill, while they chortle in unholy glee at your mystification."

100

B-10—Wonder House, Bartow, Florida

There was no limit to the imagination of attraction operators. This is the Conrad Schuck "Wonder House" in Bartow. The house featured a variety of plants incorporated into its structure as well as "unique ideas and step-saving devices." Schuck promised "a surprise at every turn."

Florida's Fairyland, Sanlando Springs, between Sanford and Orlando   237

Prior to the coming of Disney in the mid-1960s, tourists took to the highways to visit the numerous botanical and scenic gardens that dotted the Florida countryside. One favorite was Sanlando Springs, between Sanford and Orlando, which offered 100 acres of landscaped floral displays.

101

The Mead Botanical Gardens, between Orlando and Winter Park, offered a rich array of flowers. A particular emphasis was placed on the cultivation of many species and varieties of orchids.

FLAMINGO POND, PARROT JUNGLE, MIAMI, FLORIDA

Parrot Jungle in Miami combined colorfully landscaped gardens with a large collection of exotic birds, such as pink flamingos, African cranes, Amazon parrots, and white swans. Alas, such roadside gardens are a thing of the past, and many of these attractions have given way to housing developments or condominiums.

83 — The "Jose Gaspar" in Hillsborough River During Gasparilla Festival, Tampa, Fla.

Florida is also known as the "Festival State," and many locales developed specialized festivals to draw tourists into the local economy. One of the most famous festivals in the Sunshine State is the Gasparilla Festival, which centers around the exploits of the mythical pirate Jose Gaspar. So convincing is the legend of Gaspar that some residents and visitors insist the legend is true and get "fighting mad" when told the legend is pure advertising fiction.

103

State fairs, such as this one in Tampa, also drew thousands of local residents and out-of-state visitors. More recent festivals and fairs include the Strawberry Festival in Plant City, the Seafood Festival in Grant, and the Frog Leg Festival in Fellsmere, to say nothing of the Corn Festival in Zellwood and the Indian River Festival in Titusville. Other fairs, festivals, and celebrations are held in virtually every county and city in the state.

St. Petersburg, the Sunshine State's "Sunshine City," holds its week-long "Festival of States" each year. The highlight of the festival is the crowning of the festival queen.

B. 5—Baseball Spring Training—Milwaukee Braves
in Action—Bradenton, Fla.

Winter Home of MILWAUKEE BRA

Its warm climate and almost perpetual sunshine makes Florida a sports haven. From the early 1920s until today, the state has been the spring training home of many professional baseball teams, such as the Milwaukee (now Atlanta) Braves. Thousands of fans join their teams in Vero Beach, St. Petersburg, Punta Gorda, Plant City, Tampa, Viera, Auburndale, Orlando, and other cities for this annual rite of spring.

Although the first thoroughbred horse race was held in the 1840s, the Florida "boom" of the 1920s and the approval of pari-mutuel gambling by the legislature in 1931 led to the construction of both horse tracks and dog tracks in every region of the state. Tourists were among the many who attended these races. This is the famous Gulfstream Track near Miami.

Some tracks, such as Hialeah in Miami, were home to both horse and dog racing. Greyhound dogs and thoroughbred horse used the same oval track.

S6 A Blanket Finish at Hialeah Race Track, Miami, Florida

"A Blanket Finish" reads the caption for this postcard of race action at Hialeah Track in Miami. The huge board, located on the infield at the finish line, gave race results and betting payoffs to the onlookers.

The Miami Jockey Club provided its clients with the "Totalisator Board," which provided information on race entrants, betting odds, and race results for a number of tracks around the country. Many tourists came to Florida solely to enjoy the full racing season.

107

The annual "Parade of States," held at Gulfstream Park on Florida Derby Day, recognized the importance of out-of-state visitors and bettors to the continued economic well-being of the track operators.

Tropical Park, near Miami, bills itself as "the friendly park" and provides its visitors with air-conditioned comfort in several lounges and restaurants.

369   "Jai Alai" (say Hi-Li) World's Fastest Sport, Biscayne Fronton, Miami, Florida

Visitors to Florida frequently became aficionados of jai alai, pronounced "hi-li," a game imported from Cuba. Jai alai is reputed to be the fastest ball game in the world and combines elements of handball, baseball, and tennis. The strange-looking curved contraption carried by the players is known as the cesta and is used to catch and throw the ball. The first "fronton," or court, opened in 1923, and the game has been around ever since.

For tourists who wanted more active sports activities, Florida's 30,000 lakes, extended coastline, and plentiful rivers offered fishermen a great opportunity to catch a variety of fish.

Florida's lakes also provided sportsmen and women the perfect venues for such exciting sports as powerboat racing, such as this one on Lake Hollingsworth in Lakeland.

A Day's catch in the waters in front of Florida Medical Center   Venice, Florida

The warm waters of the Gulf of Mexico near Venice provided a bountiful catch for this group of happy fishermen in the 1940s.

This dandified fisherman recorded his marlin catch in 1930 in the ocean waters off the shore of Miami. With his pith helmet and white shoes, he appears dressed more for croquet than he does for serious deep-sea fishing.

111

For the wealthier "snowbirds" on Miami Beach, polo, the sport of princes, was a favorite pastime. Only the wealthy could afford to underwrite the costs of maintaining a stable of polo ponies.

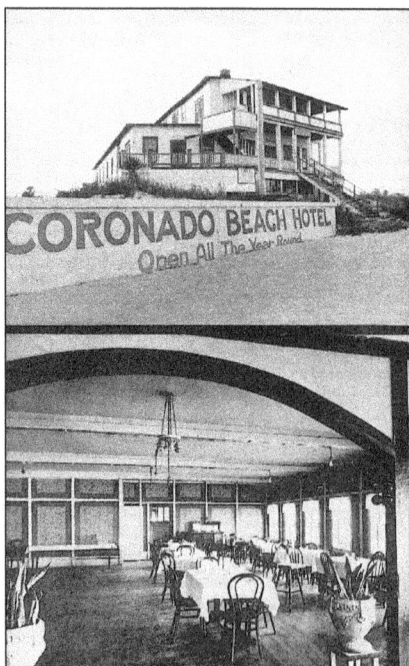

By the mid-1960s, tourism was no longer a seasonal business but had become a year-round enterprise. Large and small hotels proudly announced that they were open and ready to serve the public 12 months a year.

Tourism was so important to the economy of Florida cities that many of them established chambers of commerce to provide information and assistance. Many of these were manned 24 hours a day, seven days a week. This stately Mediterranean Revival building housed the Orlando Chamber of Commerce.

By the 1960s, Floridians realized that tourists were attracted to historical sites. The Florida Department of State began to promote such historical centers as St. Augustine and Pensacola. Pensacola's extensive fortifications, dating from the 17th century, provide the opportunity to stroll back into time and relive the excitement of all of the military history of the United States.

House Boats, Fort Myers, Fla.

An alternative to motels, hotels, tents, autocamps, and trailers is what these houseboats in Fort Myers offered to tourists who wanted to live just a little bit differently.

Ross Allen was a legendary figure in Florida's modern tourist pantheon. Operating from his reptile institute at Silver Springs, he provided countless thrills as he milked rattlesnakes. The venom collected during these shows was processed into anti-venom for use in treating victims of snakebites.

Ross Allen provides a thrilling show for visitors to Silver Springs as he captures an alligator in the crystal clear water of the springs.

For those tourists who wanted even more exotic activities, Florida offered the opportunity to hunt the deadly diamondback rattlesnake and to enjoy it as a meal.

Sarasota has been the winter home of circus performers since the early 1900s. Thousands of tourists flocked to the area to see these performers as they trained their animals and perfected their acts for the next season. Today, the Circus Museum is located on the grounds of the Ringling Mansion, named Ca'd'Zan.

Florida's extensive system of state parks provided recreational outlets for the tourists who ventured into the countryside. This 1948 Ford "woody" hauls two fishing boats to Hillsborough River State Park in Pasco County.

Old Wood Burner Locomotive in Waterfront Park
Bradenton, Florida

Small attractions like this old wood-burning locomotive in Bradenton's Waterfront Park provided interesting, but brief, stops for automobile tourists in the 1950s.

Oceanfront Promenade, Daytona Beach, Fla.

Daytona Beach's famed Promenade was as much an attraction to 1940s visitors as it is for modern-day college students on spring break. Many of the Promenade's features, such as the bandstand and needle monument, are still present today, and a visitor from the 1940s would have no difficulty recognizing the location.

Florida cities actively promoted their attractions in the 1960s, just as they did in the 1940s. This was Lakeland's entry in Tampa's Gasparilla Festival in 1962. The Polk County city bills itself as the "World's Citrus Center."

The "Conch Train" provides tourists with an up-close view of Key West, the nation's southernmost city. Long a quaint haunt for literary figures and sailors, the city was a favorite of President Harry S. Truman. Key West became a tourist destination in the early 1980s when singer Jimmy Buffett made it his home and sang songs about it.

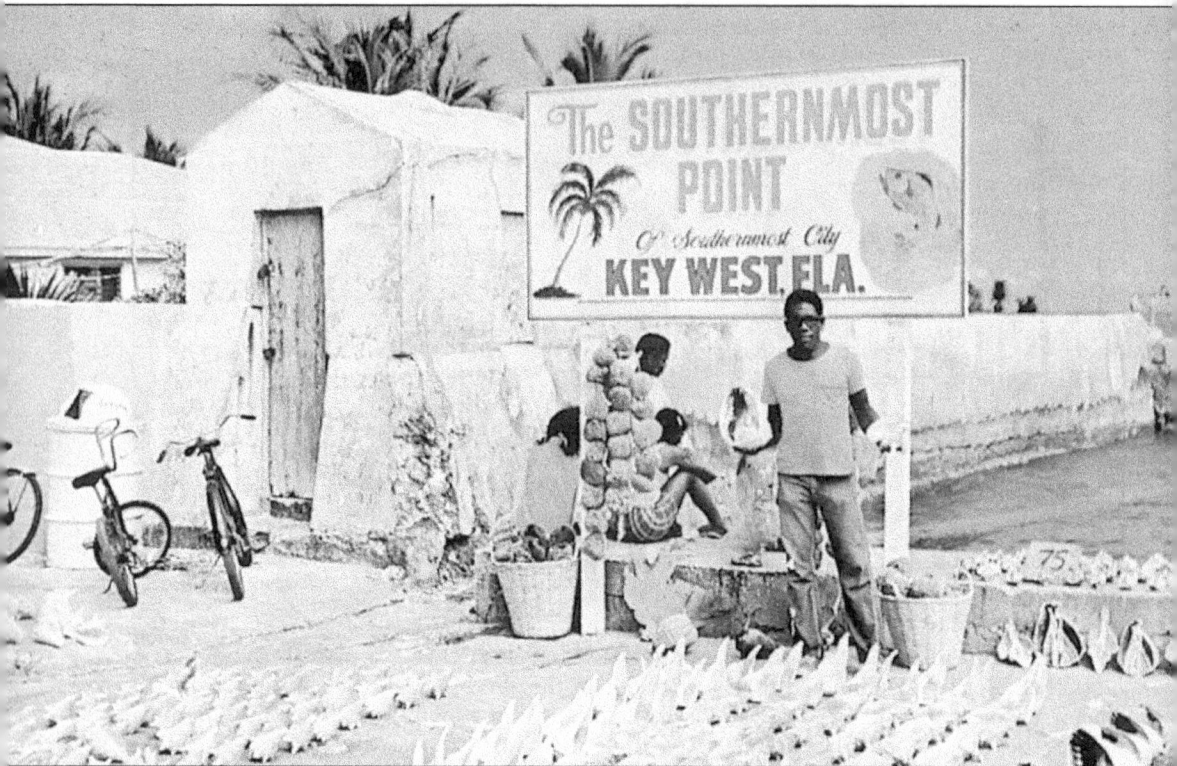

At the absolute southern end of the United States, this entrepreneur offers visitors a variety of shells and sponges as souvenirs.

By "Streamliner" Thru Tropical Florida

The end of the 1960s also saw the end of passenger train service to the Sunshine State. This form of transportation had been essential to the development of the state's tourist industry in the late 1800s and early 1900s, but interstate highways, airplanes, and the independent mindset of modern Americans spelled the end of this mode of travel. With the fixed routes and tight schedules, passenger trains were too inflexible for today's tourist.

FLORIDA GATOR				"Quicky Card"

DATE...................................	TOO BUSY TO WR...

DEAR				Thinking of You	
ARRIVED				Swimming	Loafing
Safe	Late		On Time	Sleeping	Petting
THE TRIP WAS				Fishing	Golfing
Long		Tiresome		Business	Traveling
Interesting		Fun		I SAW	
I AM STAYING AT THE				The Gulf of Mexico	
............................Quicky............				The Atlantic Ocean	
HOW ARE YOU?				The Orange Groves	
I AM				Interesting Attractions	
Fine		Happy		You in my Dreams	
Lonesome		Sad	Broke	HOPE U R	
Flying High				True 2 Me	Having F...
Enjoying the Tropics				Feeling O. K.	Missin' N...
WISH I HAD				I HAVE BEEN	
You		A Letter		Good	No Good
More Ambition				I AM	
Someone to Love Me				Well	Sick
More Sleep				Homesick	Tired
THINGS ARE				WILL LEAVE HERE	
Wonderful		Lovely		Today	Tomorro...
Exciting				Soon	
DOING LOTS OF				Yours	
Sight-Seeing					

© CURT TEICH & CO., INC.

Tourists who came to Florida were expected to be so busy enjoying the many different activities available in the Sunshine State that postcard manufacturers developed this postal "shorthand" to allow them to write to the folks at home without losing too much time. (Courtesy of the University of South Florida Library, Special Collections Department.)

Five

THE ERA OF
THE THEME PARK

1970-2000

Tourism in Florida has undergone some significant changes during the last quarter of the 20th century. Tourism today consists of two groups of individuals, neither of which is particularly interested in exploring the hinterland.

The "snowbirds" are those people who come to Florida for a minimum of six months and a day in order to qualify for resident status so that they can take advantage of the state's no-income-tax provisions and who spend the remainder of the year in northern states. Most of these tourists are collected in the high-rise condominiums located on the beaches of the Atlantic or Gulf, surrounded by tennis courts and golf courses, and are little interested in finding out about Florida's history or customs.

The second kind of modern tourist is the "day tripper," whose stay might be for a couple of weeks but whose impact on the state is calculated in terms of days. In 1969, the Florida Legislature created the Division of Tourism to coordinate and track efforts by localities, business groups, theme parks, and the hospitality industry to attract even more tourism. By 1977, more than 19 million visitors flocked to Florida. By 1980, this number had increased to more than 25 million, and of these, more than 10.6 million came by automobile. By 1987, this number had increased to 34 million, and 17.5 million arrived by automobile. The individuals who arrive by automobile, as opposed to those who arrive by airlines or other means of travel, generally tend to stay four to five days longer in the state. In 1987, for example, the average stay of a person arriving by airplane was 8.6 days, while those who arrived by automobile stayed an average of 12.8 days. Only about 25–30% of the annual influx of tourists visited the various theme parks in the state, while the remaining numbers tended to concentrate in resort areas on the beaches. The typical tourist sees little more of Florida than can be seen on the way to and from the airport or what can be seen from the interstate highways while traveling 70 to 80 miles an hour.

There are no more Ernest Meyers. There are no more Tin Canners.

Cocoa Beach, FL

Few major highways in the United States lack one or more billboards touting Ron Jon's Surf Shop in Cocoa Beach. This is a mandatory stop for visitors on Florida's east coast. Open 24 hours a day, Ron Jon's garish art deco exterior, with its bright neon lights, has become a tourist destination.

Experience Southern Hospitality in the Heart of Brevard.
Over 50 Unique Shops & Restaurants

Many small towns in Florida, such as Historic Cocoa Village, have learned that "quaintness" sells. Throughout Florida, there are hundreds of such towns that combine historic preservation, antique shops, art galleries, and small boutiques into a viable economy.

Although the three major theme parks in Florida (Disney World, Busch Gardens, and Universal Studios) account for the largest number of visitors each year, eco-tourism has provided a niche for small entrepreneurs.

The Florida wilderness is still a major attraction for visitors to the state. One of the favorite activities of tourists who have "maxed out" on the major theme parks is to take a break in the swamps and rivers.

MIDWAY AIRBOAT RIDES

ALLIGATOR FACTS

- The St. John's River is the largest river in North America that runs north. It is 285 miles long.

- Alligators swim in water at about 16 mph. They can run forty to fifty feet on dry land, faster than a galloping horse and can stay under water for 1 to 2 hours.

- If you measure from the tip of their nose to the tops of their eyes you can figure their approximate size. 1 inch equals 1 foot. 1 inch equals 1 year in age.

- The male alligator will grow to about 14 feet and can weigh approximately 700 lbs. They can live to be about 50 to 70 years of age.

- Gators will eat anything they can swallow. They don't chew.

- Alligators are reptiles that hatch from eggs and have been around for over 200 million years. All they know is eat, breed and survive.

- Bald eagles winter on the St. John's River.

28501 East Highway 50
Christmas, Florida 32709
(407) 568-6790

The alligator has been the symbol of Florida since the early visits of Jacques LeMoyne. Although on the verge of extinction in the 1960s, the alligator is a protected species and has made a remarkable comeback in the Sunshine State. The State of Florida now conducts an annual alligator hunt as a means of controlling the growing population.

JUNGLE ADVENTURES

GREATER ORLANDO · CHRISTMAS · FLORIDA

Exciting Jungle Cruise

Thousands Of Gators In Their Natural Habitat

Jungle Adventures, a small theme park located on Highway 50 near Titusville, combines Florida history, ecology, and a Native-American village. For visitors who have experienced the long lines of the major theme parks, Jungle Adventures offers few waits and personalized attention.

126

America's space program attracts hundreds of thousands of visitors each year. Tourists can view the technology used to hurl mankind into space. Each shuttle launch attracts thousands more sightseers, who line the highways and bridges in a 30-mile radius to witness this awesome display of brute power. (Courtesy of Southern Card & Novelty, Ormond Beach, Florida.)

More than eight million tourists from Asia and Europe arrive by charter flights each year in Florida. For many, the Kennedy Space Center, with its tours of actual launch sites and rockets, is a must see.

127

Simply **CYPRESS GARDENS**
WINTER HAVEN, FLORIDA

NEW
The SOUTHERN BREEZE
Cypress Gardens
See Inside.

Valuable offer inside!

Florida's First Theme Park ★ Est. 1936
Read on – you won't believe it,

Although no longer the premier attractions in Florida, older favorites like Cypress Gardens continue to attract large numbers of annual visitors.

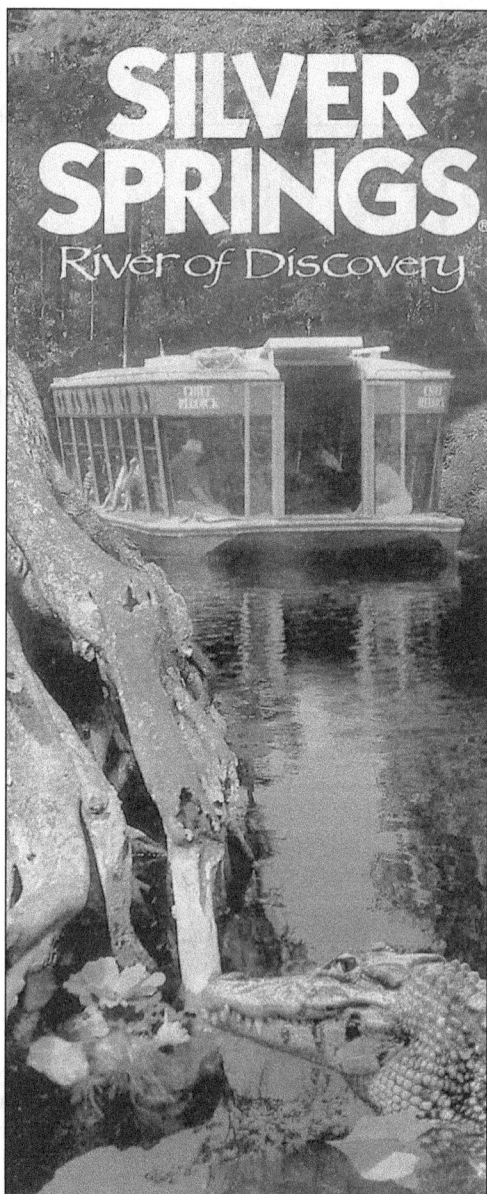

SILVER SPRINGS
River of Discovery

Silver Springs, with its crystal-clear waters, wild animals, and emphasis on nature, remains as much of an attraction for modern visitors as it did in the late 1800s when such luminaries as Presidents Ulysses S. Grant and Grover Cleveland paid visits. Chances are, the springs will be attracting new visitors in 2070.

128

Visit us at
arcadiapublishing.com

www.ingramcontent.com/pod-product-compliance
Lightning Source LLC
Chambersburg PA
CBHW080909100426
42812CB00007B/2218